You're Hopeless, CHARLIE BROWN!

by Charles M. Schulz

Selected cartoons from
YOU'RE WEIRD, SIR!
Volume 3

FAWCETT CREST • NEW YORK

A Fawcett Crest Book
Published by Ballantine Books
Contents of Book: PEANUTS ® Comic Strips by Charles M. Schulz
                    Copyright © 1981, 1982 by United Feature Syndicate, Inc.

Library of Congress Catalog Card Number: 82-81658

ISBN 0-449-20268-2

This book comprises a portion of YOU'RE WEIRD, SIR! and is reprinted by
arrangement with Holt, Rinehart & Winston.

Manufactured in the United States of America

First Ballantine Books Edition: April 1984

10 9 8 7 6 5 4 3 2 1

You're Hopeless, CHARLIE BROWN!

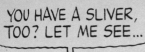

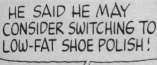

BONK!

BUMP!

BONK!

THEN AGAIN, MAYBE YOU SHOULDN'T USE QUITE SO MUCH "STICKUM"

YOU SHOULD GO OVER AND TALK WITH THAT LITTLE RED-HAIRED GIRL, CHARLIE BROWN

ASK HER TO EAT LUNCH WITH YOU

TELL HER YOU'D BE HAPPY JUST TO BE WITH HER FOR AN HOUR OR SO

AN HOUR? I'D SETTLE FOR AN "OR SO"!

YOU KNOW WHAT THE "BALANCE OF NATURE" IS?

IT'S WHAT KEEPS THE WORLD GOING... OR SO THEY SAY..

SO YOU KNOW WHO BELIEVES IN THE BALANCE OF NATURE?

THOSE WHO DON'T GET EATEN!

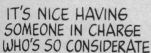

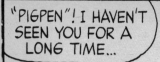

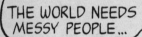

READ THIS, MARCIE...IT'S ALL ABOUT A SCHOOL FOR GIFTED CHILDREN

I'VE NEVER HEARD OF A SCHOOL BEFORE THAT GIVES YOU THINGS

I DON'T THINK IT MEANS THAT, SIR

I'D SETTLE FOR JUST A T-SHIRT

I'M GOING OVER TO THE SCHOOL FOR GIFTED CHILDREN, MARCIE... I DON'T SUPPOSE YOU WANT TO COME ALONG..

I DON'T THINK SO, SIR

I IMAGINE IT'S A LOT LIKE PLAYING IN A PRO-AM

FIRST YOU CHECK IN, AND THEN YOU PICK UP YOUR GIFTS

I DON'T THINK IT'S LIKE THAT AT ALL, SIR...

I JUST WISH I HAD KNOWN ABOUT THIS WAY BACK IN KINDERGARTEN..

SHE WENT OVER TO A SCHOOL FOR GIFTED CHILDREN, CHARLES..SHE THINKS THEY'RE GOING TO GIVE HER THINGS...

I DON'T KNOW WHAT TO DO ABOUT HER, CHARLES.. SHE NEVER LISTENS...

CHARLES? ARE YOU THERE? WHO AM I TALKING TO?

IF I BARK, IT'LL SCARE HER TO DEATH...

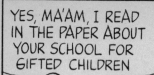

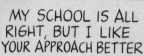

MISUNDERSTANDING? ISN'T THIS THE SCHOOL FOR GIFTED CHILDREN? AREN'T YOU GONNA FILL MY BAG WITH GIFTS?

BUT I THOUGHT... I WAS SURE THAT... AREN'T YOU... I MEAN... I...

OH, NO!

IF ANYONE ASKS FOR ME, I WAS NEVER HERE!

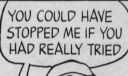

SHE'S GONE, CHARLES! PEPPERMINT PATTY HAS LEFT TOWN!

BUT I JUST TALKED TO HER YESTERDAY...

I THINK SHE WAS MORE DEPRESSED THAN WE THOUGHT, CHARLES... WHERE DO YOU THINK SHE WENT?

"SPIKE'S REAL ESTATE..NEEDLES, CALIFORNIA"...WELL, I'M NOT REALLY READY TO BUY... COULDN'T YOU JUST FIND ME A PLACE TO STAY?

CHARLIE BROWN, HAS ANYONE
EVER TOLD YOU THAT YOU
WALK FUNNY?

YOU DON'T HAVE ANY RHYTHM!
YOUR FEET POINT IN ALL THE
WRONG DIRECTIONS..YOUR ARMS
SWING THE WRONG WAY...

STAND UP STRAIGHT..NOW
MOVE FORWARD...WALK
THE WAY I TOLD YOU...

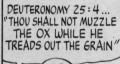

IN SOUTHWEST CAMEROON THERE ARE FROGS THAT WEIGH TEN POUNDS

THAT IS DEFINITELY NOT SOMETHING TO BE TOLD JUST BEFORE YOU GO TO SLEEP

I HAVE IT ALL FIGURED OUT, MARCIE...

THE WAY I SEE IT, THERE SEEM TO BE MORE QUESTIONS THAN THERE ARE ANSWERS

SO?

SO TRY TO BE THE ONE WHO ASKS THE QUESTIONS!

WHAT SHOULD I WRITE?

WRITE WHAT YOU FEEL

Dear Little Red-Haired Girl, I love you very much.

NOW, ALL YOU HAVE TO DO IS SLIP THE NOTE INTO THE MAIL SLOT IN THE FRONT DOOR OF HER HOUSE...

➡

HERE WE GO FOR THE FIRST HOCKEY GAME OF THE SEASON...

I CAN SEE MYSELF NOW OUT ON THE OL' POND RACING DOWN THE ICE WITH THE PUCK!

AFTER IT GETS A LITTLE COLDER

ARE YOU AWARE THAT HALLOWEEN IS COMING?

ON HALLOWEEN THE "GREAT PUMPKIN" RISES OUT OF THE PUMPKIN PATCH, AND BRINGS TOYS TO ALL THE CHILDREN IN THE WORLD!

I FIND THAT HARD TO BELIEVE

MY SWEET BABBOO SAYS IT'S TRUE

HOWEVER, I'M NOT YOUR SWEET BABBOO!

MY SWEET BABBOO SAYS IF WE SIT HERE IN THE PUMPKIN PATCH, WE MAY SEE THE "GREAT PUMPKIN"

I DON'T KNOW..

YOU CAN PROBABLY SEE A LOT OF STRANGE THINGS IN A PUMPKIN PATCH...

BONSOIR, MADEMOISELLE... IS THIS, BY CHANCE, THE ROAD TO PARIS?

SCHULZ

OKAY, MARCIE, WE'RE GONNA PRACTICE THE OL' STATUE OF LIBERTY PLAY...

YOU FADE BACK TO PASS, AND I COME RUNNING AROUND AND GRAB THE BALL

MARCIE! YOU'RE SUPPOSED TO LET GO OF THE BALL!

Gentlemen,
    Regarding the recent rejection slip you sent me.

I think there might have been a misunderstanding.

What I really wanted was for you to publish my story, and send me fifty thousand dollars.

Didn't you realize that?

WE'RE GOING TO MY GRAMMA'S TOMORROW FOR THANKSGIVING...

PUMPKIN PIE! SWEET POTATOES! EVERYTHING!

THE BEST PART, OF COURSE, IS WHEN THEY CARVE THE BIRD!

boot!
boot!
boot!

HERE ARE THE WORLD FAMOUS HOCKEY PLAYERS SKATING OUT FOR THE BIG GAME...

THEY STAND AT CENTER ICE FOR THE NATIONAL ANTHEM

WOODSTOCK ALWAYS PRETENDS HE KNOWS THE WORDS...

GUESS WHAT, CHUCK... THEY MADE MARCIE A PATROL PERSON!

CAN YOU IMAGINE THAT? CAN YOU REALLY IMAGINE THAT, CHUCK?

WELL, I DON'T KNOW... SHE'S A VERY GOOD STUDENT..I SUPPOSE SHE DESERVES IT...

I HATE TALKING TO YOU, CHUCK!

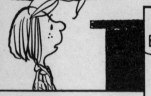

IF YOU'RE GOING TO CROSS THE STREET, PLEASE WAIT FOR YOUR SCHOOL PATROL PERSON TO HALT THE TRAFFIC...

YOU MAY NOW CROSS...

STOP

HAVE A NICE DAY, STUDENT PEDESTRIAN...

STOP

I CAN'T STAND IT!

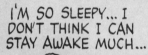

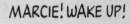

IT'S JUST TOO BAD THAT I'M ONLY A SUBSTITUTE PATROL PERSON, CHUCK...IT REALLY IS!

I'D STRAIGHTEN THINGS OUT IN A HURRY!

YOUR GRAMPA WAS AN MP IN WORLD WAR II, WASN'T HE?

THAT'S RIGHT, CHUCK, AND NO GI EVER GOT INTO THE PX BEFORE NOON WHEN **HE** WAS ON DUTY!

OKAY, BUG, YOU SAY THAT "SANTA BUG" IS COMING TO TOWN...
TELL ME THIS...AND I HATE TO ASK...
WHO IS GOING TO BE PULLING HIS SLEIGH?
EIGHT TINY REINBUGS?
SCHULZ

ONCE THEY GET SCRATCHED OFF MY CHRISTMAS LIST, THEY NEVER GET BACK!

MAJOR FUNDING FOR THIS MEAL WAS PROVIDED BY A GRANT FROM OUR FAMILY

IF THEY HAVE A PLEDGE NIGHT, I'M LEAVING!